Deadliest Reptiles

Kris Hirschmann

ReferencePoint Press®

San Diego, CA

© 2017 ReferencePoint Press, Inc.
Printed in the United States

For more information, contact:
ReferencePoint Press, Inc.
PO Box 27779
San Diego, CA 92198
www. ReferencePointPress.com

LIBRARY OF CONGRESS CATALOGING-IN-PUBLICATION DATA

Names: Hirschmann, Kris, 1967- , author.
Title: Deadliest reptiles / Kris Hirschmann.
Description: San Diego, CA : ReferencePoint Press, Inc., 2016. | Series: Deadliest predators | Includes bibliographical references and index. | Audience: Grades 9 - 12.
Identifiers: LCCN 2016004758 (print) | LCCN 2016013647 (ebook) | ISBN 9781682820520 (hardback) | ISBN 9781682820537 (eBook)
Subjects: LCSH: Dangerous reptiles--Juvenile literature.
Classification: LCC QL645.7 .H57 2016 (print) | LCC QL645.7 (ebook) | DDC 597.9--dc23
LC record available at http://lccn.loc.gov/2016004758

Contents

Introduction

A Diverse Group

Reptiles are a diverse group of animals that includes turtles, crocodilians, lizards, snakes, and the iguana-like tuatara as well as the extinct ancestors of these creatures. There are about ten thousand reptile species currently living on Earth. With about six thousand species, lizards make up the bulk of this group. Snakes come in second with about thirty-four hundred species. There are roughly four hundred turtle species, twenty-five types of crocodilians, and a smattering of other lesser-known animals.

At a glance, these groups of animals seem quite different. But they all belong in the reptile family because they share certain features. Reptiles are either four-legged or, like legless snakes, descended from four-legged ancestors. They have backbones and scaled skin, and they use lungs to breathe air. With a very few exceptions, they lay eggs instead of carrying live young inside their bodies. Almost all reptiles are cold-blooded, which means they cannot regulate their body temperature internally; instead, they rely on the environment to warm and cool themselves.

Ruthless Predators

Although reptiles are alike in many key ways, they are different in others. Whereas some reptiles are tiny, others are enormous. Some are weak; others are strong. Some have a harmless bite; others are venomous. Some are shy; others are aggressive.

In this equation, it is clearly the *others* that people need to worry about. Certain reptiles are universally feared because of their size, strength, venom, bad temper, or some combination of these qualities. Saltwater crocodiles, for example, are huge and powerful. A snake called the inland taipan is shy, but it carries one of the deadliest venom loads in the animal kingdom. The Komodo dragon is just plain hungry, and it is not intimidated at all by people. Its habit of roaming into human habitations makes this lizard a constant threat within its home range.

These dangers, of course, are not confined to humans. The world's deadliest reptiles are ruthless predators that have all the tools they need to hunt, kill, and eat a wide variety of animals, including mammals, birds, amphibians, insects, and even other reptiles. When a hungry reptile goes looking for food, its intended prey—whether large or small, whether it lives on land, in the air, or in the water—is in grave danger.

Nature in Balance

Although some reptiles are undeniably intimidating, these animals do not hunt for fun. They hunt because they need to eat. When they do, they help to maintain an ecosystem's natural balance. A snake that eats insects, for example, helps to keep bug populations from exploding out of control. Alligator snapping turtles gobble debris and carcasses from pond floors, thereby keeping their environment clean. And hungry alligators keep certain fish species in check. Without these predators, the

The Komodo dragon, which is found in Indonesia, is the largest living species of lizard. It is not intimidated by people and will wander into populated areas, which makes it a constant threat.

ecosystem would change in unpredictable and possibly harmful ways.

One example of this type of change occurred during the 1960s, when a population of crocodilians in South America plunged to critical levels. The area's piranha population exploded as a result. These meat-eating fish, which are known for biting mammals that enter the water, posed a danger to human swimmers over a wide area. As the crocodilians recovered, the piranhas were subjected to greater and greater predation, and their population soon dropped back to normal levels.

Reptiles in Danger

This story helps to illustrate the importance of reptile conservation efforts. In this particular case, international laws were passed to protect the endangered South American crocodilian, which was being hunted for its skin. The laws made it illegal to harvest or sell the animal's hide. This ban eliminated most crocodile hunting and allowed populations to recover.

This success story, though, is not the general rule. Many reptile populations are threatened today by human harvesting, habitat loss, or a combination of both. A study done in 2013 by the Zoological Society of London in conjunction with the International Union for Conservation of Nature (IUCN) surveyed fifteen hundred reptile species to determine their population health. The study showed that 19 percent, or about one in five species, were threatened with extinction. The biggest problem was habitat loss due to farming and deforestation. Reptile harvesting and pressure from invasive species (non-native animals introduced into an area) also played important roles.

These problems, unfortunately, are not easy to solve. Earth's growing human population requires more and more resources, so farming and deforestation will continue. Invasive species, once established in a new area, are nearly impossible to remove. And harvesting of reptile products can be forbidden, but illegal poaching continues. For a species already on the brink of extinction, even a little poaching might be too much.

Worthy of Respect

Still, it is important to try. Reptiles and other creatures that give people the chills have their place in the natural order. Understanding this fact will not make people stop fearing them, of course, and this is not a bad thing. A little bit of healthy fear might stop someone from grabbing a venomous snake, stepping near a snapping turtle's head, or swimming too close to a crocodile. Creatures of such power deserve respect and a cautious approach.

As long as the proper care is taken, though, there is no reason people cannot appreciate even the most dangerous reptiles—from a safe distance. And those who choose to can learn more about reptiles and gain the knowledge and the confidence to get closer. By understanding these remarkable creatures, they can safely give them the admiration they so richly deserve.

Chapter 1

Saltwater Crocodile

Saltwater crocodiles—or salties, as they are informally called—are the biggest and heaviest reptiles on Earth. These massive beasts are the planet's largest land and river predators. With ample power and speed to back up their huge size, saltwater crocodiles dominate every environment in which they live. They pose a constant threat to all creatures that venture into their territories, including humans.

Body Basics

Saltwater crocodiles are classified in the Crocodylia scientific order along with alligators, caimans, and gharials. Like all members of this group, saltwater crocodiles have four strong legs that stick out from the sides of a thick central body. Their tails are long and flexible and are flattened into a sharp ridge on top. Their heads are large and strong, with two eyes bulging up from the area above the skull plate. The animal's overall color is usually a dark greenish gray, although some individuals have lighter skin. Some saltwater crocodiles are even tan with darker spots or bars.

The shape of the saltwater crocodile's head has some subtle differences that distinguish it from other crocodilians. The snout is long and wide compared to the snouts of most crocodiles. It is roughly triangular, narrowing from a broad rear to a rounded point at the tip. Two bony ridges run back along the head, starting behind the crocodile's protruding eyes. The skin on top of the head is bumpy and dark, but the skin on the bottom—under the crocodile's chin and on its throat—is smooth and lighter in color.

All of these features provide useful clues to the saltwater crocodile's identity. The best clue of all, though, is simply this animal's enormous size, which is unmatched by any other member of the crocodile family. Adult male salties regularly reach lengths of more than 17 feet (5.2 m) and often weigh over 2,000 pounds (909 kg), but some individuals are larger—much larger. The biggest saltwater crocodile ever accurately measured was 20 feet, 8 inches (6.3 m) long and weighed about 3,000 pounds (1,360 kg). Currently, an even larger individual is said to live in Bhitarkanika Park, a wildlife preserve in eastern India. The record-breaking croc has not been formally measured, but it is reputed to be 23 feet, 4 inches (7.1 m) long and weigh about 4,400 pounds (2,000 kg).

Built Tough

The saltwater crocodile is not only huge but also immensely strong and tough. Its body has many built-in protections and weapons that make this animal nearly indestructible.

The crocodile's skin is the first line of defense. Saltwater crocodiles are sheathed in a covering of structures called scutes. Scutes are like scales and serve the same function, but they form deeper in the skin out of harder materials. They blanket the crocodile's entire body and stop virtually any natural object—such as the sharp teeth

Saltwater crocodiles are Earth's largest land and river predators. Their massive size and quick speed make them a constant threat to all creatures that venture into their territories, including humans.

and claws of other large predators—from penetrating to the crocodile's soft inner body. Some special scutes with bony bases, called osteoderms, poke up to form lumpy, bumpy rows down the crocodile's back. These bumps are obstacles that make it even harder for potential enemies to get a good grip.

If a creature tries to bite a saltwater crocodile despite this intimidating armor, it will have to contend with the crocodile's powerful tail. The tail is long, thick, and packed with muscles that make it viciously strong. It is also lined with two rows of hard, upward-pointing spikes. The crocodile can whip this weapon back and forth with

THE SALTWATER CROCODILE AT A GLANCE

- Scientific name: *Crocodylus porosus*
- Scientific order: Crocodylia
- Range: From the east coast of India to northern Australia and all areas in between
- Habitat: Inland swamps and lagoons, open sea
- Average size: 17 feet (5.2 m)
- Diet: Fish, reptiles, birds, large and small mammals
- Life span: Seventy years
- Key features: Massive size
- Deadly because: Huge, strong, and fast
- Conservation status: Least concern

terrifying speed, if the need arises. It does not have good aim—but accuracy is not important. The crocodile is so strong that if it lands any blow, no matter how glancing, it can severely injure its opponent.

The crocodile's mighty mouth can do even more damage. Saltwater crocodiles have massive biting power thanks to enormous, rock-hard cheek muscles that bulge out from either side of the head. The jaws are large and lined with sixty-six peg-shaped teeth, the longest of which are up to 3.5 inches (9 cm) long. The teeth do not have deep roots and often fall out when the crocodile bites. But the saltwater crocodile replaces its teeth constantly, up to fifty times in its lifetime, so a few missing teeth are no problem for this fearsome reptile.

Home and Habits

Changing from one type of water to another is no problem either. Whereas most crocodilians are freshwater dwellers, the saltwater crocodile—as its name suggests—is also comfortable in oceans. It is often found along coastlines and sometimes even ventures far out to sea in its home range, which stretches from northern Australia to southeastern Asia and east to India.

Wherever its ocean range touches land, the saltie ventures inland as well. These animals make themselves at home in freshwater swamps, lagoons, and lower stretches of rivers as well as in brackish (mixed salty

The jaws of a saltwater crocodile are lined with sixty-six peg-shaped teeth that can be several inches long. These teeth often fall out when the crocodile bites, but the saltwater crocodile replaces its teeth constantly.

and freshwater) estuaries. Inland spots are prime territory for crocodiles because of the greater prey quantity and variety. These areas are usually claimed by very large male crocodiles that can chase off their competition. It is therefore common to see the biggest saltwater crocodiles inland while smaller individuals are forced into the less desirable ocean waters.

Like all reptiles, saltwater crocodiles are cold-blooded. This means they cannot regulate their own body temperature; instead, they get warmer and cooler along with their environment. For this reason, salties often emerge from the water in the morning to bask in the sun's rays and warm their chilly bodies. They rest on riverbanks and along pond edges until their internal temperature rises to a comfortable point. Then they reenter the water. They surface and submerge repeatedly throughout the day to regulate their temperature and stay comfortable.

On the Hunt

By the time evening approaches, saltwater crocodiles have warmed themselves thoroughly. They are ready to start hunting for food. The type of food does not matter much to the saltwater crocodile. These reptiles will eat anything they can catch, including fish, lizards, amphibians, birds, and mammals. The crocodile's size determines its prey choice. Small crocodiles typically pursue small prey. The biggest crocodiles will attack just about any animal that ventures too close to the water's edge, up to and including monkeys, wild boar, and even water buffalo.

To catch these animals, salties submerge themselves in water, leaving just their eyes and nostrils poking out. They swim toward a potential meal slowly and quietly, not leaving even a ripple to betray their presence. Soon they

RECORD-BREAKING BITE

The saltwater crocodile has the strongest chomping strength of any animal on Earth. It can bite down with a pressure of up to 7,700 pounds (3,493 kg) per square inch. That is about four times the force of the strongest non-crocodilian animal, the hippopotamus, and more than fifty times stronger than a human bite. A big saltie can easily use its teeth and jaws to crush the skull of a water buffalo or another large prey animal.

The saltie gets its biting power from its strong cheek muscles. These muscles, though, are designed mostly to close the jaws, not to open them. The crocodile therefore has very little opening power. People can restrain this reptile's mighty mouth with a few loops of duct tape. Keeping the mouth firmly shut protects human handlers from bites—but many other dangers remain. Even with the mouth immobilized, the crocodile can still do plenty of damage with its whipping tail and thrashing body. When it comes to a creature this big and powerful, safety is never guaranteed.

are within striking range. They gather their strength and then use their legs and tails to thrust themselves out of the water in one mighty, lightning-quick lunge. Jaws gaping, they bridge the gap between themselves and their prey. They sink their teeth into the unlucky animal and drag it back into the water before it even has a chance to react.

Once the prey enters the water, it has little chance of survival. The crocodile pulls the prey below the surface and holds it fast. It may use its huge body to crush the prey at the same time. Held tight, with no way to breathe, the prey soon drowns. When it does, the crocodile releases its grip and settles down to eat its meal, one toothy bite at a time.

Human Attacks

Unfortunately for the human population, this technique works just as well on people as it does on animals— and the saltwater crocodile does not hesitate to attack, kill, and eat humans who venture into its territory. No one can say with certainty how many of these encounters occur each year. Recent studies, though, claim that salties attack about 30 humans annually, and death is often the result. In Australia alone, one survey attributed 106 human deaths to saltwater crocodile attacks between 1971 and 2013.

Experts point out that saltwater crocodiles attack people for two main reasons. The first type of attack is predatory, which means the crocodile is looking for a meal. In these cases, the crocodile intends to kill—and it usually succeeds. People seldom survive predatory attacks. The second type of attack involves territorial defense. Saltwater crocodiles are fiercely protective of their ranges, and they will try to drive off any potential threat. A saltie may therefore attack a human intruder just to scare him or her away. People can still be killed in these encounters, but they are much more likely to survive than victims of predatory attacks.

An environmentalist named Val Plumwood famously survived a territorial attack in 1985. Plumwood was canoeing in Australia's Kakadu National Park when she noticed a large saltwater crocodile swimming toward her boat. She did not expect any trouble—so, she recalls, "I was totally unprepared for the great blow when it struck the canoe. . . . The unheard of was happening; the canoe was under attack!"[1]

During the terrifying encounter that followed, Plumwood was pulled from her canoe and mauled nearly to death. But thanks to a timely rescue and skilled medical care, this explorer survived—barely—to tell her story.

Expanding Range

This cautionary tale has become more relevant than ever in recent years. Thanks to laws that protect saltwater crocodiles, these animals are now in the midst

Saltwater crocodiles catch their prey by leaping from the water and sinking their teeth into the animal, dragging it back into the water before it can react. Here, a saltwater crocodile attacks a pig.

of a population explosion. There are an estimated two hundred thousand salties in Australia alone, and hundreds of thousands more in other countries. And because saltwater crocodiles prefer to live far away from one another, this growing population is spreading quickly into new territories, including many human-inhabited regions.

Even areas once thought to be crocodile-free may not be safe. In 2010, for example, a tourist named Lauren Failla was attacked and killed by a 12-foot (4 m) crocodile while scuba diving on an Indian coral reef. The attack, said authorities, "was considered to be an extremely unlikely event, given that it took place in open water over a coral reef, in an area lacking any mangrove refuse in the vicinity, [near a] popular beach . . . where no crocodile has ever been sighted before."[2] Unlikely, perhaps—but not impossible, as this story clearly shows.

No Safe Place

Authorities do their best to minimize crocodile-related tragedies like this one. They post signs in known saltie areas warning people to stay away. Sometimes they also trap nuisance crocodiles and move them to remote areas.

But these efforts can only do so much. Signs only work if people see them and obey them. Relocated crocodiles often find their way back home—and even if the old crocs do not return, new ones soon move in to claim the vacant territory. An area that is safe and crocodile-free one day can turn into a deadly hunting ground overnight. When it comes to these predators, the only way to keep safe is to stay away—far, far away—from places where they are likely to roam.

Chapter 2

Reticulated Python

Snakes are among the most dreaded creatures in the reptile family, and with good reason. These animals are silent, skilled, and ruthless hunters. All thirty-four hundred snake species share these qualities—but among this fearsome group, one species stands out simply because it is so shockingly large. As the world's longest snake, the reticulated python seems to go on and on, stretching out as long as a limousine. That is the length of five adult humans lying end to end.

There is no doubt that a python this big is a terrifying sight, and it is potentially a fatal one as well. Reticulated pythons are active, aggressive, and ill-tempered. They are strong enough to hunt and kill prey up to one-quarter their own length, which means that people are definitely on the menu. These snakes pose a deadly threat to nearly any creature that enters their territory.

Body Basics

The reticulated python gets its name from its colors. The word *reticulated* means "netlike," and it refers to the complex geometric patterns this snake bears on its skin. The specific patterns and colors vary greatly between individuals, but the back generally is marked with a series of irregular diamond-shaped blotches that range from brown to tan to yellow in color. The blotches are outlined in a darker color, making it look a bit like a net has been thrown over the snake's body. Smaller blotches in various colors line the snake's sides.

Together, all of these markings mimic the fallen leaves and dappled sunshine found in the snake's environment. They act as camouflage, making the python hard to see. This type of camouflage is known as disruptive coloration because it disrupts the animal's body outline. At a glance, other animals—and people—often do not notice the reticulated python basking on the ground.

This hiding ability is remarkable considering this snake's enormous size. Reticulated pythons regularly reach lengths over 20 feet (6 m) and weights of more than 200 pounds (91 kg). But they can get even bigger—*much* bigger. Over the past two hundred years there have been many published reports of 30-foot-plus (9 m) monsters.

These reports may or may not be accurate. Although reticulated pythons of such staggering size may indeed have been spotted, they have not been measured carefully. This means no one can be certain of their true length. Officially, the largest-ever python is Medusa, a captive snake that lives in Kansas City, Missouri. When measured in October 2011, this reptile was found to be 25 feet, 2 inches (7.7 m) long, with a weight of 350 pounds (159 kg). Fifteen men had to stretch Medusa out to her full length in order for this measurement to be taken.

Home and Habits

Captive pythons like Medusa can be found in zoos and other facilities all over the world. In the wild, though, reticulated pythons are limited to a much smaller range. These reptiles are native to Southeast Asia, from Indochina through the Philippines. They sometimes settle in woodlands and grasslands but strongly prefer tropical rain forests where average temperatures range from about 80° to 92°F (27° to 33°C). They are excellent swimmers and are often found near rivers, ponds, and other bodies of water.

Reticulated pythons are nocturnal. This means they are active during the night. They spend the daytime hours resting in trees or on the ground. Only when dusk arrives do they begin to stir. They open their round eyes, which are a striking deep orange with black, vertical slits for pupils. They look around for signs of prey.

The reticulated python, the world's longest snake, has netlike markings and coloration that mimic the environment, camouflaging the snake and making it difficult to see despite its enormous size.

THE RETICULATED PYTHON
AT A GLANCE

- **Scientific name:** *Python reticulatus*
- **Scientific order:** Squamata
- **Range:** Southeast Asia, including Indochina, Indonesia, and the Philippines
- **Habitat:** Tropical rain forests
- **Length:** Up to 30 feet (9 m)
- **Diet:** Mammals and birds
- **Life span:** Up to twenty-nine years
- **Key features:** Massive length
- **Deadly because:** Squeezes prey to death
- **Conservation status:** Vulnerable

Often there is no prey in sight, and the python decides to seek a better location. It moves off, heaving its bulk forward in a straight line rather than in a side-to-side motion. It does this by stiffening its ribs to provide support, then moving a set of belly scales forward to grip the ground and pull. By repeating this process over and over, the snake moves forward slowly, with a top speed of about 1 mile per hour (1.6 km/h). Little by little the snake makes its way across its territory.

On the Hunt

As the reticulated python travels, it uses its sharp eyes to look for rustling grass and leaves that might hide prey. It flicks its forked tongue in and out of its mouth. The tongue collects scent particles from the air and deposits them in the snake's scent organ, which is located on the roof of the mouth. The python also uses heat-sensing pits on its jaw to detect the body heat of buried or hidden animals.

The prey pursued depends on the snake's size. Smaller pythons look mostly for signs left by small- to medium-size prey, such as rodents, monkeys, birds, and lizards. Larger pythons will pursue bigger prey, including wallabies, pigs, antelope, and even leopards. Pythons are usually careful to select victims they are confident they can handle. If prey is scarce, though, hunger may drive them to make poor choices. "Snakes have been known to swallow adult male antelope with horns and all and die in the process," explains one expert. "They'll take whatever they can get if they are desperately hungry."[3]

The reticulated python sleeps during the day and wakes up at night to hunt for prey, using its excellent vision. Its round eyes are a striking deep orange with black, vertical slits for pupils.

DEADLY PETS

It is legal to keep reticulated pythons as pets in many countries. These pets are spectacular but potentially deadly. A python that escapes from its tank can attack and even kill its owners. One such incident occurred in 2008, when a Virginia woman died after being strangled by her pet python. Another incident took place in Nevada in 2009, when a toddler narrowly dodged death after his mother attacked a constricting 18-foot (5.5 m) pet python with a knife. The wounded snake released the boy, who at that point was turning blue from oxygen loss.

Securely caged pythons are dangerous too. Snake experts point out that in the wild, reticulated pythons stay rock-still for long periods and then explode into action when the need arises. Pet pythons may seem passive, but they have this frightening ability, just like their wild relatives do. Inexperienced python owners can be lulled into a false sense of security by a seemingly tame, calm snake—but one wrong move may push the "sleepy" reptile into an attack. For this reason and many others, only experienced snake handlers should attempt to keep pythons.

Desperate or not, a python eventually finds evidence that prey is nearby. When this happens, the snake settles down and rests, still but alert. It watches and waits for prey to approach. It may wait on land, or it may enter a river or pond and lurk near the edge with just its eyes and nostrils showing.

If the python is lucky, an unwary animal will soon come too close. When it does, the snake strikes. It shoots its large head forward with its jaws gaping open to reveal rows of long, curved, backward-pointing teeth. It bites the prey hard, driving its teeth deep into the flesh. The bite is not venomous and does not make the prey sick— but that does not matter. The python is much too big and powerful for most creatures to escape. Its strong jaws and buried teeth act like a vise grip to hold the prey tight.

As the snake's victim struggles helplessly, the python's mighty body springs into action. It coils itself around and around the prey. The number of coils depends on the size of the prey. The bigger the creature, the more coils the reticulated python uses to hold it tight.

Squeezed to Death

Once the prey is securely trapped, the snake starts to tighten its coils. This process is called constriction, and snakes that use it are called constrictors. The python squeezes harder and harder, crushing the life out of its prey.

Until recently, scientists believed that the reticulated python and other constrictors killed their prey by suffocation—squeezing them so tightly that they could not expand their lungs to get a breath. New studies, though, have found that this is not the case. Scientists now know that constriction puts so much pressure on the blood vessels that the heart can no longer push blood through the body. As a result, vital organs shut down within minutes.

The python is acutely aware of this process. It can feel its victim's heart hammering madly as it squeezes. It also feels the heart faltering and then stopping. Only when the last spark of life disappears does the snake loosen its fatal grip and pull its teeth loose from the victim's body.

The python then shifts its body, bringing its head in line with the prey's head. It opens its mouth wide, stretching the ligaments of its jaws to create a vast, gaping maw. It slides the jaws around the prey's head and digs its teeth back into the flesh. Then it starts working its jaws back and forth—left, right, left, right. With each shift, the curved teeth pull the prey a little bit deeper into the python's throat. The prey slowly slides into the snake, forming a huge lump in the serpent's midsection. The snake then begins the process of digesting its prey, which can take anywhere from a few hours to ten weeks, depending on the size of the meal.

Hungry for Humans

Snake expert Tom Kessenich recalls vividly the moment he almost became such a meal. The man was handling a captive python when the snake struck. It dug its teeth into Kessenich's forearm. Within three to five seconds, he recalls, the snake "wrapped around my upper torso and neck. . . . I could still breathe, but it was hard. The pressure was unbelievable."[4] Kessenich tried but failed to pry the snake loose. He finally managed to escape by submerging his attacker's head under running water from a bathroom tap, surprising it into releasing its grip.

Television personality Brady Barr also knows firsthand how strong the reticulated python can be. In 2007 Barr was wading through waist-deep muck in an Indonesian cave with his film crew when an angry 13-foot (3.9 m) python dug its teeth into his left leg. "I was so completely incapacitated by the pain, I couldn't even attempt to

Once a reticulated python has caught an animal, it coils itself around and around its prey. Then the python tightens its coils, squeezing harder and harder until it crushes the life out of its victim.

remove the snake from my leg. I was super scared that the snake was going to pull me off my feet with its coils around my legs and drag me underwater," Barr recalls. "The power of these snakes is beyond comprehension."[5] The snake eventually released its grip, leaving Barr with a series of bone-deep gashes that took months to heal.

Kessenich and Barr were lucky to survive their python encounters. Other people, however, have been less fortunate. The reticulated python is fully capable of subduing and eating human children and small adults, and it does so occasionally in its native habitats. In 1995, for instance, a 23-foot (7 m) reticulated python squeezed a man to death in southern Malaysia. And recent interviews with the Agta tribe, a hunter-gatherer group that lives alongside pythons in the Philippine rain forest, reveal that six tribespeople have been killed by these reptiles over a thirty-nine-year period. This number includes two children who were eaten by one very hungry snake on a single night.

Further information from the Agta interview shows a shocking pattern of human predation. A full 26 percent of the men in this six-hundred-member tribe say they have been attacked by pythons. This data suggests that reticulated pythons do not just attack people under rare conditions. They view humans as tasty treats and will eat them if they can. This snake clearly has all of the tools it needs to hunt and slay large animals—and practically any creature, including careless humans, can end up on this deadly predator's menu.

Chapter 3

Komodo Dragon

There are about six thousand lizard species on Earth. Of these, one type stretches head and tail beyond the rest in terms of both its size and its deadly potential. Found only on five islands in southeastern Indonesia— Komodo, Rinca, Flores, Gili Motang, and Gili Dasami— the intimidating Komodo dragon can grow to more than 10 feet (3 m) long and can weigh up to 366 pounds (166 kg). That is about the length and weight of two adult humans put together. This huge creature has an appetite and an attitude to match its fearsome size. It is no wonder the Komodo dragon has a well-deserved reputation as one of the world's deadliest reptiles.

Body Basics

The Komodo dragon gets its name from its appearance, which some people consider a bit dragon-like. This lizard has a thick, scaly central body ending in a long tail that tapers to a point. The body is supported by four sturdy legs. When walking, the lizard holds its legs straight beneath its body. When it rests, the legs splay out to the sides in typical lizard fashion. Each leg ends in a padded, five-toed foot. The toes have long, curved, black claws that the Komodo dragon uses for fighting, digging, climbing, and hunting.

The entire body is covered with thick, wrinkled skin that is mostly gray and brown in color but may also contain hints of yellow, green, pink, and other shades. Small, overlapping scales cover the skin smoothly. These scales act like built-in armor to protect the Komodo dragon's tender insides from harm.

The Komodo dragon's head, too, is covered with smooth scales. The head is oval in shape. Two prominent nostrils sit at the front of the snout. The lizard's eyes, which are round and deep black, sit farther back on the head. Brow ridges arch over each eye, creating a subtle forehead.

The Komodo dragon walks on four sturdy legs that end in a padded, five-toed foot. The dragon's toes have long, curved black claws that are useful for fighting, digging, climbing, and hunting.

The Komodo dragon's large mouth runs nearly the length of its head. A long, forked, yellow tongue flicks in and out of the mouth occasionally. When the mouth opens wide, the dragon reveals about sixty teeth, each measuring up to 1 inch (2.5 cm) long. The teeth are serrated, which means their edges are jagged, like knives. They tear out fairly easily during feeding, but the Komodo dragon soon grows back any teeth it has lost.

The Komodo dragon's gums are unusually fleshy. They grow up, around, and sometimes even right over the lizard's teeth. This soft tissue is constantly being torn and broken while the dragon eats. It never fully heals, which means that countless small wounds weep blood into the Komodo dragon's mouth most of the time. For this reason, the lizard's saliva is usually tinged from pink to red, depending on the amount of blood it carries.

Home and Habits

The islands where Komodo dragons live are volcanic in origin. They are small, rugged, and hilly. Habitats range from forests to grasslands and beaches to mountains. Komodo dragons generally prefer grassy areas and forests, but some individuals choose different homes. It is not uncommon to find dragons living along the seashore or on high mountain ridges.

Within their home ranges, most Komodo dragons retreat to burrows or dens when they want to rest. Sometimes they dig these burrows themselves, using their strong forelegs and long claws to scratch shallow trenches in the ground. At other times they may take over the abandoned dens of other dragons. Some dragons prefer to take shelter between tree roots, under rocks, or even in old human shelters rather than using burrows.

A Komodo dragon's burrow has two main uses. During the hottest daytime hours, which often reach temperatures over 95°F (35°C), dragons use their burrows to take shelter from the heat. At night, when temperatures plunge, a burrow keeps its owner warm.

When morning arrives, Komodo dragons emerge from their resting places. Like all reptiles, these animals are cold-blooded and must warm up before they can be active. A Komodo dragon therefore spends some time basking in the morning sunlight each day. Thanks to its cozy burrow, the lizard has not lost too much body heat during the night, and it can warm itself quickly. The dragon reaches the peak of its energy by early afternoon. When this moment arrives, the hungry lizard is ready to go on the hunt.

On the Hunt

Komodo dragons are not choosy about their food. They will eat just about anything they can catch. Young dragons pursue small prey, including insects, geckos, eggs, and little mammals, such as rats and mice. Larger dragons can subdue bigger prey and will go after monkeys, deer, goats, boar, and even water buffalo. In addition to live prey, Komodo dragons will also eat any dead animals they happen to find lying around.

Komodo dragons are mostly ambush hunters. They rest quietly in the long grass next to game trails, waiting for animals to wander past. When an unsuspecting creature comes too close, the dragon erupts from its hiding place, jaws agape. It buries its jagged teeth in the prey's flesh and then uses its curved claws to further maul its victim. It readjusts its bite, if it gets the chance, to deliver a killing crunch to the prey's soft throat.

THE KOMODO DRAGON AT A GLANCE

- **Scientific name:** *Varanus komodoensis*
- **Scientific order:** Squamata
- **Range:** Southeastern Indonesia
- **Habitat:** Open grasslands and tropical forests
- **Average size:** 8.5 feet (2.6 m)
- **Diet:** Nearly any live or dead animal
- **Life span:** Thirty years or more
- **Key features:** World's largest lizard
- **Deadly because:** Strength and toxic bite
- **Conservation status:** Vulnerable

This technique often fails, though, and the Komodo dragon's prey may escape between bites. The wounded animal flees from its attacker. The dragon is capable of short bursts of speed up to 12 miles per hour (19.3 km/h) and may follow for a short distance. But deer and other nimble prey can easily outrun their slower pursuer. The Komodo dragon will not get its meal—for now.

Bacterial Bite

But all is not yet lost. The Komodo dragon's bloody bite delivers a toxic cocktail into the prey's flesh. This lizard's saliva contains more than twenty types of lethal bacteria. Some researchers believe the saliva also includes a mild venom that causes reduced blood clotting, low blood pressure, and muscle weakness, although this has not been proven.

The head of the Komodo dragon is covered with smooth scales and features round, deep black eyes and two prominent nostrils. The dragon's mouth runs nearly the length of its head, with a long, flicking, forked tongue.

Whatever its precise content, the saliva goes to work immediately to sicken the wounded prey. The animal becomes weaker and weaker over a period of several days. It eventually dies from a combination of its flesh wounds and the toxins in its body. As the dead animal begins to decompose, its corpse gives off pungent gases that waft throughout the surrounding area. This odor is like a dinner bell for nearby Komodo dragons. These animals have an excellent sense of smell and can detect the scent of dead flesh from about 2.5 miles (4 km) away. They do not smell with their nostrils but rather with their tongues. The forked tongue collects scent particles from the air and deposits them in an organ on the roof of the mouth. The organ analyzes the scent information to figure out the dead animal's identity, distance, and precise location.

As the delicious odor spreads, many Komodo dragons approach. The group may or may not include the dragon responsible for the kill. It does not really matter. However the prey died, it is available now—and the hungry lizards are ready to eat.

Big Eaters

The Komodo dragons settle in for their meal. They use their knifelike teeth to tear off huge hunks of flesh and bone, then gobble them down whole. The dragons eat nearly every part of the prey, with the exception of undigested material inside the corpse's guts. They shake the intestines back and forth vigorously to empty them before gulping them down.

When a single Komodo dragon snags a smaller meal, the process is different. Komodo dragons have loosely hinged jaws and flexible skulls that allow them to swallow prey bigger than their own heads. The dragon opens wide and rams the prey down its throat, sometimes pushing it against a tree or rock for leverage. Muscles in the throat pull the meal into the dragon's expandable

UNPREDICTABLE ATTACK

Perhaps the best-known Komodo dragon attack occurred in 2001, when Hollywood actress Sharon Stone arranged for her husband, Phil Bronstein, to see one of these lizards firsthand at the Los Angeles Zoo. The zookeeper invited Bronstein to enter the animal's cage, explaining that the dragon was very mild mannered and safe to visit.

Bronstein accepted the invitation and stepped into the cage after removing his white shoes, which the keeper worried might remind the Komodo dragon of tasty white rats. Unfortunately, Bronstein's bare feet seemed to have the same effect. The dragon took a few exploratory sniffs. Then it opened its jaws, lunged, and chomped down on Bronstein's foot. It started to whip its head back and forth, attempting to rip off the appendage. Bronstein reached down and managed to wrench the dragon's jaws loose, but the top half of his foot was gone.

This incident spotlights the Komodo dragon's unpredictable nature. Even if these animals seem sluggish and tame most of the time, they are predators at heart. No one can predict when or where they may get the urge to attack.

stomach, sometimes creating a visible bulge in the lizard's belly.

A single Komodo dragon can eat up to 80 percent of its own body weight in one sitting. After this vast meal has been consumed, the bloated dragon retreats to a sunny spot to bask and digest its food. The digestion process can take up to five days. When it is done, the dragon vomits a slime-covered pellet containing the prey's bones, teeth, claws, and other unusable material. The meal is now complete, and the Komodo dragon is ready to begin its next hunt.

Komodo dragons use their knifelike teeth to tear off huge hunks of flesh and bone, which they gobble down whole. Here, two Komodo dragons feast on a dead dolphin.

Human Encounters

This hunt might include any type of prey, including humans. Although Komodo dragons seldom pursue people actively, they are not intimidated by them either. They will happily attack any person who strays into their territory.

One such incident occurred in 2007 in a state park on the island of Komodo, when an eight-year-old boy left a scrubland path to take a bathroom break. The boy and his friends did not know that a Komodo dragon was lying in ambush at that precise spot. Seeing its chance, the dragon lunged. "The Komodo bit him on his waist and tossed him viciously from side to side," a park spokesman later reported. "The boy's uncle threw rocks at the lizard until it let go and fled."[6] Unfortunately, the rescue came too late for the victim, who died from massive bleeding about thirty minutes later.

A Rinca Island resident named Maen narrowly escaped the same fate. Maen was just sitting down in his office when he discovered that a Komodo dragon had crept into the room during the night and was sheltering below the desk. Maen tried to pull his legs and feet to safety, but the lizard was too quick; it clamped its jaws around Maen's calf. Maen shouted for help—with terrifying results. "All the people come running here, but other dragons follow along as well,"[7] he recalled later. The rescuers had to fight off not only the attacking dragon but also the hungry reptile horde to get Maen to safety.

These stories are not isolated incidents. Humans who live on the islands where Komodo dragons roam come into frequent contact with these reptiles. Attacks are not common, but they do occur—and when they do, death is sometimes the result. Extreme caution is necessary when living among these deadly predators.

Chapter 4

Alligator Snapping Turtle

In a discussion about deadly creatures, turtles are not necessarily the first animals that leap to mind. These reptiles have a reputation for being slow and gentle. But turtles are predators, and a member of the turtle family called the alligator snapping turtle is exceptionally large, powerful, and good at this job. Alligator snappers are quick enough and strong enough to capture all sorts of prey, both in and out of the water. They cannot kill large animals or humans, but they will attack if threatened—and their bite can do serious harm. Wherever they are found, these creatures are worthy of caution and respect.

Body Basics

Sheer size is part of the reason alligator snapping turtles are so powerful. These creatures are among the world's largest freshwater turtles, second only to one rare Vietnamese species. Alligator snappers grow throughout their lifetimes, so their size depends largely on their age. Older individuals often have shells over 3 feet (.9 m) long and weigh between 155 and 175 pounds (70 and 80 kg)—but some specimens are much larger. The biggest alligator snapper ever found weighed a reported 403 pounds (183 kg). Other large individuals include a 249-pound (113 kg) turtle that lived at Chicago's Shedd

THE ALLIGATOR SNAPPING TURTLE AT A GLANCE

- **Scientific name:** *Macrochelys temminckii*
- **Scientific order:** Testudinae
- **Range:** Southeastern United States
- **Habitat:** Muddy swamps, lakes, and rivers
- **Average size:** 3 feet (.9 m)
- **Diet:** Fish, frogs, turtles, and carrion
- **Life span:** Up to seventy years
- **Key features:** Prehistoric armored appearance
- **Deadly because:** Strong bite and bad temper
- **Conservation status:** Threatened

Aquarium until 1999 and a 236-pound (107 kg) resident of the Brookfield Zoo, also in Chicago.

Whatever their size, all alligator snapping turtles share certain physical features. Their back consists of a thick, hard shell made of bony scutes. Some of the scutes are raised and pointed. These raised scales are arranged in three ridges that run from the front of the shell to the rear. The outer edge of the shell is knobby and jagged. The belly is covered by smooth scutes that connect to the upper shell by thin bridges, forming a solid case around the turtle's middle section.

The alligator snapper's legs, tail, and head stick out of this case. The legs are strong and sturdy. The long tail is thick at the base and tapers to a point. The head is rounded and very big compared to the rest of the turtle's body. It is mounted on a neck that the turtle can shorten or stretch out as needed. This neck, along with the rest of the turtle's exposed body parts, is covered with leathery skin that, while not as strong as shell material, still provides protection against injury or attack.

Alligator snapping turtles are among the world's largest freshwater turtles. Their strength and speed allow them to catch prey both in and out of the water. Although they cannot kill large animals or humans, their bite can do serious harm.

Living Dinosaurs

Between its large size and all of this protective covering, the alligator snapping turtle is a bit like a four-legged, living tank. It is so heavily armored that it looks not so much like a modern animal but rather like something that might have lived millions of years ago. One woman who found an alligator snapper along a river remembers how she and her friends reacted. "When we saw it, we did not even realize that it was a turtle. It reminded us of a dinosaur,"[8] she said in a newspaper report.

The alligator snapper's lumpy, bumpy shell, which resembles the bony back plates of some dinosaurs, is largely responsible for giving people this impression. But this turtle has many other features that add to its prehistoric look. The reptile's feet, for example, bear thick, bony claws that would look right at home on an ancient predator. The skin of the legs, head, and tail is deeply wrinkled and covered with wartlike knobs. The round, protruding eyes are yellowish and surrounded by small, fleshy appendages, like eyelashes made of skin.

At the very tip of the alligator snapping turtle's head is a wicked-looking beak, with a downward-pointing spike on the top and an upward-pointing spike on the bottom. When the turtle shuts its mouth, the opposing spikes come together like a crab's pinching claw. This feature, which was shared by the long-extinct triceratops and some other dinosaurs, adds to the alligator snapping turtle's ancient appearance.

Home and Habits

In the wild, people do not often get the chance to marvel at this creature's looks. The alligator snapping turtle

THE BEAST OF BUSCO

Residents of the small town of Churubusco, Indiana, claim that a local pond called Fulk Lake once sheltered the largest alligator snapping turtle ever to live. There were five reported sightings of the Beast of Busco, as this reptile is known, between 1948 and 1949. The turtle was said to have a shell as big as the top of a car, a neck the size of a stovepipe, and a head the size of a child's.

Gale Harris, the farmer who owned the pond where the Beast was allegedly spotted, went to great efforts to find the monstrous turtle. He set traps for the creature and hired divers to search the pond. When these attempts failed, he rigged up a pump to drain the 7-acre (3 ha) reservoir. The job was almost done—still with no sign of the Beast—when torrential rains struck, refilling the pond. After this setback, Harris gave up in disgust and sold his farm.

There has been no sign of the Beast of Busco since 1949. Experts believe, however, that a snapping turtle this big could exist. Maybe the Beast—or its remains, at least—does indeed rest at the bottom of Fulk Lake. The truth will be revealed only if or when the pond finally dries up.

spends almost all of its time underwater in the swamps, lakes, and rivers of its home range, which stretches across the southeastern United States. It does not emerge to sun itself on exposed rocks and tree branches, as most turtles do. Alligator snappers do breathe air and must surface occasionally to fill their lungs, but they can go hours between breaths. And when they do breathe, they still do not surface completely; they stick just their nostrils out of the water. They take a quick gasp of air, then sink back down into the watery depths.

Even if a person entered the water, alligator snapping turtles would still be hard to spot. These animals rest in the most secluded places they can find, nestling their big bodies among tree roots, under overhanging riverbanks, or within forests of underwater growth. "Information about the turtle is very difficult to collect in the wild because the turtle is so secretive and so elusive. . . . It inhabits all the places where nobody wants to go,"[9] ex-

The back of an alligator snapper consists of a thick, hard shell made of bony scutes arranged in ridges. The turtle's legs are strong and sturdy, and its head is very large in comparison to the rest of its body.

plains a turtle farmer who has been working with these reptiles for decades.

Alligator snapping turtles also stay very still most of the time—yet another habit that helps these creatures to avoid attracting attention. They move so little, in fact, that their shells often sprout thick, hairy mats of algae. The green growth blends perfectly with underwater vegetation, camouflaging these turtles and making them even harder to see.

On the Hunt

This disguise comes in handy when it is time for an alligator snapping turtle to hunt for food. Resting motionless, the algae-covered turtle looks like a big rock. Potential prey do not realize that this "rock" is actually a stealthy predator, waiting in ambush for a tasty meal to come too close.

This meal might include just about any type of animal. Alligator snapping turtles are voracious meat eaters that will gobble down underwater prey such as fish, mollusks, frogs, snakes, worms, and other turtles with enthusiasm. They are equally happy with a meal of carrion and will eat any type of dead animal that falls into the water. In captivity, alligator snapping turtles also eat some fruits and vegetables, but they prefer meat above all other foods.

To get this meat, alligator snappers use a unique built-in lure that attracts prey. The lure is actually the turtle's long, pink tongue, which looks like a worm. A hunting turtle opens its mouth wide and wiggles this tongue while holding the rest of its body perfectly still. The squirming tongue catches the attention of nearby fish and other animals, which dart over to investigate.

If the turtle is lucky, the curious creature may decide to take a closer look.

When this happens, the turtle springs into action. It straightens its neck to shoot its head forward with alarming speed. It bites down on the prey with all its might, plunging the spikes of its bony beak into the prey's flesh and clamping down with its rock-hard jaw bones. This bite is powerful enough to snap a wooden broom handle in half—and it does devastating damage to the much thinner bones of its prey. The victim, which is injured much too severely to escape, is gobbled down whole by the hungry turtle.

Encounters with Humans

As an ambush hunter, the alligator snapping turtle does not actively pursue prey, and it will not chase people who enter the water. This does not mean, though, that human swimmers are safe from alligator snappers. These turtles are known for being bad-tempered and quick to snap at anybody or anything that gets too close. A person who accidentally steps near one of these reptiles runs the risk of being bitten.

An alligator snapping turtle's bite will not kill a human, but it can do significant damage. There have been many tales over the years of people losing fingers and toes during encounters with this animal. In 2013 an alligator snapper bit and severed an eight-year-old swimmer's Achilles's tendon in a popular lake. A public panic followed, and the lake was drained in an effort—ultimately unsuccessful—to find the reptilian offender.

Wild alligator snappers are not the only threat to people. Captive turtles also may attack people if they are not handled with extreme caution. Zoo employees understand this risk and know how to keep themselves safe around alligator snapping turtles. People who keep alligator snappers as pets, though, do not always have the same level of knowledge. These amateurs may underestimate the alligator snapper's speed, flexibility, or power. They sometimes receive nasty bites as a result.

An incident from 2014 illustrates this danger. In March of that year, one man got a shock when he leaned in to give a stray alligator snapper a gentle kiss—and promptly had his upper lip impaled by the irritated creature. It took several people to pry the turtle loose after it refused to release its grip. The bleeding man ended up in the hospital, where he received treatment for his mangled mouth.

The alligator snapper uses its pink, wormlike tongue as a lure to attract prey, wiggling it until a fish or other animal comes over to investigate. Then the turtle clamps its powerful jaws down on its victim, which it swallows whole.

Invasive Species

Partly because of incidents like this one, it is illegal to keep alligator snapping turtles as pets in many places. They are simply too dangerous for amateur handlers. Yet there is a bigger reason to restrict the spread of these animals: pet alligator snappers are often released into the wild when they get too large and too vicious for their owners to handle. These reptiles have no trouble surviving outside their home range, and they happily settle down anywhere they find themselves. If males and females were released in the same area, they could establish a breeding population and take over formerly turtle-free waters.

So far, this is not known to have happened. But individual alligator snappers have shown up in some very far-flung spots. In recent years these turtles have been found in China, Bavaria, Russia, Oregon, and New York, to name just a few sightings. Some of these places have strict laws against keeping alligator snappers—but obviously the laws have been broken.

Officials are trying their hardest to stop this practice, but some people will undoubtedly continue to keep alligator snapping turtles illegally. These reptiles are fascinating creatures, and exotic pet owners are drawn to them despite the dangers they pose. In the wild, too, people will continue to be thrilled by the occasional glimpse of this elusive animal. They can admire these oddly appealing creatures—from a safe distance.

Chapter 5

American Alligator

From dry land, the marshes and watery swamplands of the southeastern United States look still and serene. This calm surface, however, hides a deadly secret. The American alligator—one of the world's most dangerous reptiles—lurks within these placid waters, waiting for the right moment to attack and feed. In an instant, one of these animals can transform a quiet waterway into a churning, thrashing battleground that spells death for an unlucky victim.

Body Basics

Like their relatives the crocodiles, alligators are members of the crocodilian family. The American alligator is one of just two alligator species in the world. The other species, the Chinese alligator, is found only in eastern China.

American alligators, often simply called gators, are smaller than saltwater crocodiles—but not much. Gators are impressively large animals that grow to average sizes between 11 and 14 feet (3.4 and 4.3 m). The weight depends on the length but may reach more than 1,000 pounds (455 kg) in extremely big individuals.

In rare cases, measurements can even exceed these limits. There have been many sightings of gators reported to be 16 to 20 feet (4.9 to 6.1 m) long. Without official measurements, these sightings cannot be confirmed, but they are definitely plausible. A 19-foot (5.8 m) beast was killed in Louisiana in 1890, and a gator measuring over 17 feet (5.2 m) was once captured in the Florida Everglades. These events prove that monstrous alligators are not merely myths. Although rare, these creatures do indeed exist.

Whatever their size, American alligators share certain physical features. Like other crocodilians, they have armored bodies protected by bony scales. Some of the scales are sharply ridged and arranged in rows that run down the alligator's back. The long tail is flattened on top where it joins the body and is ridged along both side edges. About midway down the tail's length, the two ridges join to make one single, jagged peak that continues to the tip of the tail. The four strong legs are also scaled, as is the head. The round eyes are set close together at the top rear of the snout, which is broad and toothy.

Most adult alligators are dark in color. The shade of this animal's upper side may range from nearly black to dark gray, olive green, or brown. The belly is lighter, ranging from light brown to cream. The scales of the belly are much wider and smoother than the back scales.

Home and Habits

American alligators are common throughout the waters of the lower southeastern United States in Florida, Georgia, Alabama, Mississippi, Louisiana, and eastern Texas. Their range also stretches northward into the eastern halves of South and North Carolina. Marshes, swamps, ponds, and lakes are their preferred habitat. Alligators will also populate rivers if the water flow is not too swift. Their bodies do not tolerate saltwater well, so they are

The American alligator's massive size and speed make it one of the world's most dangerous reptiles. Here, a group of American alligators rests on a riverbank.

less common in brackish waters, and they seldom enter the ocean.

Unlike some other crocodilians, American alligators are not overly territorial. Young gators in particular are very tolerant of one another, so some areas have very high concentrations of these animals. Older, larger male gators do sometimes defend prime territories, but this behavior is uncommon among smaller individuals.

Even in highly populated areas, each alligator creates its own resting spot that it returns to again and again. A gator uses its tail, clawed feet, and snout to dig a depression—called an alligator hole—in soft, marshy ground. The depression fills with water, forming a comfortable private pool for its owner. The alligator uses the

THE AMERICAN ALLIGATOR AT A GLANCE

- **Scientific name:** *Alligator mississippiensis*
- **Scientific order:** Crocodylia
- **Range:** Southeastern United States
- **Habitat:** Swamps, marshes, and lakes
- **Average size:** 12 feet (3.7 m)
- **Diet:** Fish, birds, turtles, snakes, mammals
- **Life span:** Fifty years
- **Key features:** Broad snout, short legs, bulging belly
- **Deadly because:** Strong bite; quick and aggressive
- **Conservation status:** Least concern

pool for shelter and also to regulate its body temperature. On hot days, the water cools the alligator's body. When temperatures plunge, the water keeps the gator from getting too cold.

Although alligators may rest alone, they can stay in contact with one another while they do. These reptiles are very vocal and often bellow to announce their territories, to find mates, to signal distress, or to threaten any perceived attackers. An alligator's bellow includes a frequency called infrasound. It is too low-pitched for human ears to hear, but it can be felt throughout the body as a deep rumbling sensation. A loud infrasound bellow sends out shock waves that make the water around the alligator's body ripple in an effect known as a water dance.

On the Hunt

This type of vocalization may be handy in certain situations. When the time comes to hunt, though, silence is critical. The alligator must make as little noise as possible to avoid scaring off prey. This is no problem for alligators, which swish their tails back and forth to propel themselves gracefully through the water. They use muscles inside their bodies to shift their lungs around, like balloons, to change their buoyancy and sometimes their direction. By using this internal steering mechanism, they keep their limbs still and their position level. The water barely ripples as they glide forward.

The back of an American alligator features bony scales called scutes, which are sharply ridged and arranged in rows. These scales provide protection and help keep the alligator warm.

KEYSTONE SPECIES

Animals that are critical to the health of their environments are called keystone species. American alligators have earned this title due to their habit of digging alligator holes. Over time, an alligator-heavy area becomes pockmarked with these depressions as thousands upon thousands of gators make themselves comfortable. A gator hole can measure up to 20 feet (6 m) across. Under typical conditions, these holes fill with water to form tiny ponds. The ponds provide water for many animals and all sorts of plants.

Gator holes are even more important when droughts strike. During these periods, swampy areas may dry up—but the gator holes remain. Fish, certain plants, and other water-dwelling organisms take shelter in these ponds while the dry conditions persist. When wetter conditions return, they emerge from the gator holes to repopulate the environment. Without this refuge, certain animals would not survive, and the ecosystem as a whole would suffer.

A hungry alligator will eat many different things. Water-dwelling creatures, especially fish, are the most common meals. Other menu items include turtles, frogs, lizards, and snakes. Alligators will also eat land-dwelling creatures, including birds and mammals, if they get the chance. To capture these animals, they either lie in ambush at the water's edge or leave the water entirely and hide in bushes or grass. The size of the prey usually depends on the size of the alligator, with larger individuals pursuing larger prey.

Whatever prey it takes, a gator's main tools are its speed and strength. In the water, an alligator uses its tail to propel itself forward quickly. On land, it runs on its four sturdy legs. It cannot run for long distances, but it can be shockingly quick over short stretches. A lunging gator can reach an intended victim before the animal has enough time to react.

It lunges with its mouth wide open, baring up to eighty peg-like teeth. The alligator crushes its jaws closed with incredible force, driving these teeth into the prey's flesh and holding it tight. Bones and shells crack as the predator bites down harder and harder.

What happens next depends on the prey. Small prey is killed nearly instantly and can be gobbled down whole. Larger prey, however, may require more effort. To subdue big animals, particularly land-living creatures, an alligator drags the prey underwater. It spins or flails its body wildly, over and over, with its teeth still embedded in the prey's flesh. The force of this motion rips away bite-sized chunks of the victim's body. Called a death roll, this behavior usually finishes off animals that survive the alligator's initial bite.

Human Encounters

Humans do not often find themselves in this situation. Alligators seldom attack people, even though these reptiles are common in human-inhabited areas. In murky water, though, an alligator may mistake a person's arm or leg for a tasty fish. The alligator bites—and even though the prey is not what it expected, the hungry animal will do its best to finish the job.

A woman named Rachael Lilienthal survived an attack of this type in September 2015. Lilienthal and some friends were kayaking on a serene central Florida waterway when they decided to take a cooling dip in the river. With no warning, a 9-foot (2.7 m) gator struck, digging its teeth into Lilienthal's right arm. It pulled the woman underwater and started to spin. "It rolled me around and I could feel my arm break," Lilienthal recalled later. Suddenly, unexpectedly, Lilienthal broke free of the gator's grip. She reached desperately toward her friends—who immediately saw, to their shock, exactly how the woman had managed to escape. "She tried to grab onto the kayak with her right arm, but there was no arm there," one of Lilienthal's companions explained. "It got completely ripped off."[10]

In the end, Lilienthal's friends managed to pull her out of the water and summon medical attention. Thanks to their quick action, the woman survived her alligator encounter. Others, however, have not been so lucky. In 2015 alone, three people—two in Florida and one in Texas—were killed by alligators. Many others were attacked but survived to tell the tale. Such incidents are sure to continue as long as people and alligators frequent the same areas.

Nuisance Gators

This type of interaction has become more and more common over the past several decades as alligator populations have exploded. This growth is the result of laws that were passed in the late 1960s to protect gators, which were then in danger of extinction. This is no longer the case. Numbering an estimated 5 million indi-

A hunting alligator will lunge for its prey with its mouth wide open, then crush the startled animal in its forceful jaws, driving its peg-like teeth into the prey's flesh and cracking bones and shells with its powerful bite.

viduals, the American alligator population is now considered to be fully recovered.

This recovery is a huge success for conservationists. But it has caused some problems for people who live in alligator-infested areas. Gators are unpredictable and dangerous around people. And even if they are not inclined to attack humans, a pet dog or cat is a different matter. These bite-sized animals are tempting treats for alligators that live near human populations.

To keep people and their pets safe, alligators that stray too far into civilization are often removed and killed by government organizations. These animals are called nuisance alligators. In 2014 alone, the state of Florida received 13,599 complaints about nuisance alligators. In response, it removed nearly 7,000 of these creatures.

Seven thousand alligators, though, is a tiny amount compared to a population of 5 million. The vast majority of gators cause no trouble—for people, anyway. But the alligator's natural prey undoubtedly has a different perspective. Fish, birds, small mammals, and other creatures that share the American alligator's territory will always be in danger from this deadly predator.

Chapter 6

Inland Taipan

A reptile does not have to be big or strong to be lethal. It just needs the right tools—and the inland taipan of Australia definitely has what it takes to get the job done. Also known as the small-scaled snake or the fierce snake, this creature has by far the deadliest venom of any reptile on Earth. The toxins delivered in a single bite could kill up to one hundred adult humans. With this impressive killing power, the inland taipan poses a mortal danger to any living creature that enters its range.

Body Basics

The inland taipan's rather plain body gives no hint about the danger lurking inside. This reptile is slightly but not remarkably large for a snake—adults are usually about 5 to 6 feet (1.5 to 1.8 m) long, which is about as long as an adult human's height. Individuals sometimes grow longer, up to a maximum of more than 8 feet (2.4 m), but shorter lengths are more typical. The build is medium, neither slender nor thick, although it tends a bit toward the stocky side. The snake's head is rectangular in shape, but not strongly so, and it is about the same width as the rest of the body.

The inland taipan's color depends on the time of year. During warm seasons, the snake's small scales are tan

59

to olive with blackish edges. The way the scales align creates dark V-shaped marks on the snake's body. During cold seasons, the snake's scales darken to a deep brown all over. The smooth head is darker than the body, ranging from dark brown during the summer to a shiny black during the winter. The round eyes are medium in size and a deep brownish black.

Inside the taipan's mouth are the snake's deadly fangs. The fangs are short, only .25 to .5 inches (.64 to 1.3 cm) long, and they are hollow. They work like hypodermic needles to inject venom into the flesh of the snake's prey.

Home and Habits

The inland taipan lives and hunts in a remote part of central Australia. In this semiarid region, known as the black soil plains, the climate is hot and dry most of the time. Plant life is sparse, and the ground is dry and cracked. It is a hostile environment—but the inland taipan manages not only to survive but also to thrive here. Although good population counts do not exist, scientists believe that the inland taipan is plentiful in its home territory.

There are a couple of reasons why these snakes are so hard to count. The remoteness of the inland taipan's range is one reason. Additionally, these snakes seldom emerge during the midday and evening hours. They are active only in the early morning, before the day gets too hot. As the sun rises and the black soil plains start to bake in the bright sunlight, the snakes retreat into deep cracks and abandoned rodent burrows. They rest through the heat of the day and all through the night. At the first light of dawn, they rouse themselves for another burst of outdoor activity.

On the Hunt

Most of this activity involves hunting. The inland taipan slithers over and through the cracked ground looking for rats, mice, and other small mammals to eat. It will occasionally eat a bird if no other prey is available, but this is not a favorite meal.

The inland taipan's hunting patterns vary depending on the season. During certain times of the year, rat and mouse populations explode on the black soil plains. The snakes take full advantage of this bonanza. They hunt and eat often, and their bodies become thicker and heavier. When rodent populations subside, so does the inland taipan's activity level. The snake hunts and eats less, and it becomes thinner. It rests to save its energy until rodent populations rise once again.

Although the inland taipan of Australia has a rather plain body and only a medium build, it has the deadliest venom of any reptile on Earth.

THE INLAND TAIPAN
AT A GLANCE

- **Scientific name:** *Oxyuranus microlepidotus*
- **Scientific order:** Squamata
- **Range:** Central-eastern Australia
- **Habitat:** Black soil plains in dry regions
- **Average size:** 6 feet (1.8 m)
- **Diet:** Small rodents
- **Life span:** Up to twenty years
- **Key features:** Small, smooth scales
- **Deadly because:** Most toxic venom of any reptile
- **Conservation status:** Least concern

Whether it is a time of feast or famine, the inland taipan's hunting techniques stay the same. The snake moves quickly across its territory searching for prey. It looks around with its keen eyes, searching for the slightest hint of motion. It also flicks its tongue in and out. The tongue collects scent particles from the air and deposits them in the snake's scent organ, which is located on the roof of the mouth.

As soon as the inland taipan sees or smells prey, the hunt is on. The snake makes no attempt to hide or to ambush its intended victim. It simply follows the animal into the ground and chases it through the maze of underground cracks. Sooner or later the rodent finds itself backed into a corner with nowhere to run.

When this happens, the inland taipan seizes its chance. It opens its mouth, bares its needle-sharp fangs, and strikes repeatedly—up to eight times in a row. With each strike, the snake plunges its fangs into the prey's flesh and injects up to 100 milligrams of venom.

Sometimes the snake wraps its body around its prey as it delivers these bites to keep the prey from escaping. Most venomous snakes will not do this. They back off between strikes to avoid being scratched or bitten by struggling prey. The venom of the inland taipan, though, is so devastatingly powerful that it paralyzes mice and rats almost instantly. It goes to work with lightning speed to immobilize the prey, which is then gulped down whole, headfirst, by its hungry attacker.

This skull of an inland taipan reveals the snake's fangs, which are small and hollow. The snake uses its fangs to inject deadly venom into the flesh of its prey.

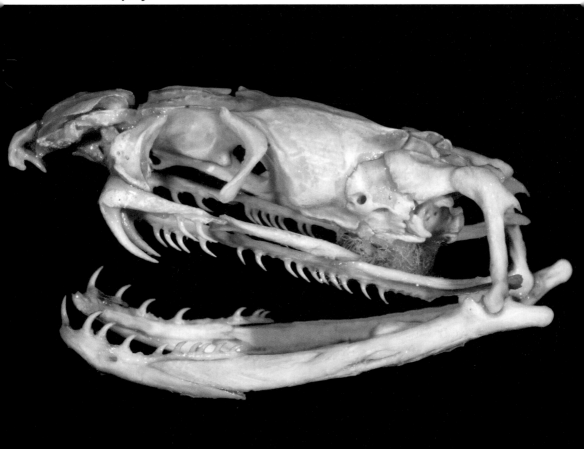

Vicious Venom

Scientists have studied the venom of the inland taipan to learn why it is so lethal. The answer lies in the fact that this snake's venom includes a mixture of poisons with different effects. Some of these poisons, for instance, work to paralyze the central nervous system. Others affect the blood and muscles. Still others affect the kidneys and the blood vessels. To top it all off, the venom also contains a substance that helps the body quickly absorb these poisons.

This cocktail of toxins has a dramatic effect on the inland taipan's victims. It overwhelms the snake's typical small targets almost instantly. Larger targets, such as humans, do not succumb quite as quickly—but the effects are felt immediately. The victim develops a splitting headache, nausea, abdominal pain, and dizziness as the venom spreads throughout the body. The muscles weaken, and breathing becomes difficult. "Effectively what it will do is it will start shutting down the function of messages going to your brain, to your vital organs, your lungs and your heart and even your muscles,"[11] explains Julie Mendezona, head reptile keeper at the Australian Reptile Park near Sydney, Australia.

Once this shutdown begins, it is hard to stop. The symptoms progress until the bite victim becomes completely paralyzed. At this point convulsions, organ failure, and death are not far behind. From beginning to end, the whole process might take as little as forty-five minutes.

These facts are bad enough on their own. But there is yet another reason to fear the inland taipan. Most venomous snakes deliver a high percentage of so-called dry bites, or bites that do not inject venom. The inland

SPECIALIZED VENOM

Venom is just a toxic type of saliva. Its recipe is highly variable from one creature to another. Each species has its own unique venom, developed over millions of years to be toxic to that particular animal's prey.

In the case of the inland taipan, the venom has adapted to be especially deadly to mice and rats. These small rodents are mammals. This means their bodies are chemically similar to those of humans, which are also mammals. This is why the inland taipan's venom is so lethal to people. It might not work as well on, say, a fish or an insect.

But there is no question that it does work well on its intended targets. A single attack from an inland taipan delivers enough venom to kill hundreds of thousands of rodents. This amount of poisoning power might seem excessive, but it is an adaptation that helps the inland taipan to survive. By subduing its prey quickly, this snake manages to thrive in a sparse and challenging habitat.

taipan, however, injects venom 100 percent of the time. This means that no one gets lucky when attacked by this reptile. Each and every time it occurs, the bite of the inland taipan is a life-threatening emergency.

Deadly but Calm

Thankfully for the human population, such emergencies are rare. This is partly because the inland taipan lives in remote areas where people seldom go. But it is also partly due to the inland taipan's personality. This snake is calm and nonaggressive, and it would much rather hide than fight. If people do enter its territory, it will lie still and let them pass if it does not feel endangered.

Like any animal, though, the inland taipan will defend itself if it feels angry or afraid. If a person corners or threatens an inland taipan, the snake responds by curling itself tightly. It raises the front part of its body in a tight S shape with the head pointing directly toward the

The inland taipan tends to be calm and nonaggressive, preferring to hide rather than to fight. The snake will lie still and allow humans to pass by if it feels safe, but it will defend itself if it feels threatened.

intruder. This position is called a threat display. It is the snake's way of showing its alarm and telling visitors to back off—now.

If a person ignores this message and comes too close, the snake will launch itself forward in attack, using its tightly coiled body like a spring. It is quick and accurate. It can complete a strike and inject its venom within a fraction of a second. It then slithers away to safety before the human victim even realizes what is happening.

A handful of people have been attacked in this way over the years. Incredibly, though, all known human victims have survived thanks to prompt treatment with antivenom, a medicine that counteracts the inland taipan's toxins. Some victims have experienced lasting effects, including heart and muscle problems, from the inland taipan's bite. But at least they are alive.

In terms of its deadly potential, then, the inland taipan is the worst of the worst—but it poses little real threat to people. As one snake expert says, "Sure, it has lethal venom with the potential to kill humans, but there is a world of difference between potentiality and reality."[12] It is a lucky break for the human population that this lethal reptile prefers to keep its distance.

Source Notes

Chapter 1: Saltwater Crocodile

1. Val Plumwood, "Surviving a Crocodile Attack," *Utne Reader,* July/August 2000. www.utne.com.
2. Quoted in Kevin Coughlin, "Lauren's Companion: 'I Did Everything in My Power to Save Her' from Crocodile; Expert Praises His Courage, and Issues Report," NJ.com, May 15, 2010. www.nj.com.

Chapter 2: Reticulated Python

3. Quoted in Ker Than, "Strangulation of Sleeping Boys Puts Spotlight on Pythons," National Geographic News, August 6, 2013. www.news.nationalgeographic.com.
4. Quoted in Peter Martin, "To Be Constricted by a Python," *Esquire*, June 29, 2006. www.esquire.com.
5. Brady Barr, "Snakebit!," Welcome to the World of Dr. Brady Barr!, July 29, 2007. http://bradybarr.com.

Chapter 3: Komodo Dragon

6. Quoted in Fred Attewill, "Boy Killed in Dragon Attack," *Guardian*, June 4, 2007. www.theguardian.com.
7. Quoted in Rachel Nuwer, "The Most Infamous Komodo Dragon Attacks of the Past 10 Years," *Smithsonian*, January 24, 2013. www.smithsonianmag.com.

Chapter 4: Alligator Snapping Turtle

8. Quoted in Ed Mazza, "The 'Dinosaur Turtle' That Freaked Everyone Out Is an Alligator Snapping Turtle," Huffington Post, July 2, 2015. www.huffington post.com.
9. Quoted in Phil Hoebing, "The Turtle in Missouri Folklore," Missouri Folklore Society, March 6, 2002. http://missourifolkloresociety.truman.edu.

Chapter 5: American Alligator

10. Quoted in Linsey Davis, "When Alligator Attacked, Rachael Lilienthal Decided to Pray," ABC News, September 29, 2015. http://abcnews.go.com.

Chapter 6: Inland Taipan

11. Quoted in Dan Proudman and Stephanie Gardiner, "Snake-Bite Victim Could Have Been Dead in 45 Minutes," *Sydney Morning Herald* Online, September 28, 2012. www.smh.com.au.
12. Brandon Cornett, "Most Venomous Snake—Meet the Inland Taipan," Reptile Knowledge, 2015. www.reptileknowledge.com.

ambush: A type of hunting in which the hunter hides and waits for prey to approach rather than actively pursuing prey.

antivenom: A medicine that counteracts the effects of snake venom. Also called antivenin.

camouflage: Colors or patterns that help an animal to blend into its surroundings.

carrion: Dead and rotting animal flesh.

cold-blooded: Having a body temperature that varies with the environment; unable to internally regulate body temperature.

constriction: Using the body to squeeze prey to death.

constrictor: A snake that uses constriction to kill prey.

death roll: An underwater spin performed by an alligator or crocodile to kill or rip apart prey.

ecosystem: A community of interacting creatures and their environment.

habitat: The natural home or environment of an animal.

infrasound: Sound pitched below the range of human hearing.

keystone species: A species that plays a critical role in how an ecosystem functions.

nocturnal: Active mostly at night.

osteoderm: A bony plate in the skin.

scutes: Bony, horny back scales or broad, flattened belly scales

toxin: A poisonous substance produced by a living thing.

venom: A poisonous liquid made by many creatures, including some reptiles, that is injected by biting or stinging.

Books

Dianna Dorisi-Winget, *Wild About Snakes: Pythons*. North Mankato, MN: Capstone, 2011.

Dorling Kindersley, *Smithsonian Nature Guide: Snakes and Other Reptiles and Amphibians*. New York: Dorling Kindersley, 2014.

Rebecca A. Hirsch, *American Alligators: Armored Roaring Reptiles*. New York: Lerner, 2015.

Rebecca A. Hirsch, *Komodo Dragons: Deadly Hunting Reptiles*. New York: Lerner, 2015.

Chris Mattison, *What Reptile? A Buyer's Guide for Reptiles and Amphibians*. Hauppauge, NY: Barron's, 2013.

Susan Schafer, *Giant Animals: Saltwater Crocodiles*. New York: Cavendish Square, 2014.

Marilyn Singer, *Venom*. Minneapolis: Millbrook, 2014.

Websites

Crocodilians: Natural History & Conservation (www .crocodilian.com). The world's largest crocodilian site has many useful databases packed with accurate information on all crocodilian species.

Discover Life (www.discoverlife.org). This site includes an electronic lizard identification guide that helps users to identify species they spot in their backyards or in the field.

Planet Deadly (www.planetdeadly.com). If something is dangerous or deadly in any way, it is probably profiled on this site.

Reptiles **Magazine** (www.reptilesmagazine.com). Oriented toward pet owners, this site includes easy-to-access information on every possible reptilian pet.

Snaketype (www.snaketype.com). Browse this site to find photos, facts, and information about many snake species.

Turtle Conservancy (www.turtleconservancy.org). This organization celebrates turtles of all types and works to save endangered species.

Index

Picture Credits

Cover: Shutterstock.com/defpicture

6: Depositphotos

11: © Will Troyer/Visuals Unlimited/Corbis

13: © Martin Harvey/Corbis

17: © Mike Parry/Minden Pictures

21: © Nick Garbutt/SuperStock/Corbis

23: © Nick Garbutt/NPL/Minden Pictures

27: ANT Photo Library/Science Source

30: © Mike Lane/FLPA/Minden Pictures

34: Depositphotos

37: © Reinhard Dirscherl/FLPA/Minden Pictures

41: © Barry Mansell/NPL/Minden Pictures

44: Europics/Newscom

47: © Linda Lewis/FLPA/Minden Pictures

51: Heidi & Hans-Juergen Koch/Minden Pictures

53: David Hosking/Minden Pictures

57: © Donald M. Jones/Minden Pictures

61: © NHPA/Photoshot

63: © NHPA/Photoshot

66: Thinkstock Images

About the Author

Kris Hirschmann has written more than three hundred books for children. She owns and runs a business that provides a variety of writing and editorial services. She lives near Orlando, Florida, with her husband, Michael, and her daughters, Nikki and Erika.